SAINTS ALIVE!

created by

☆margaret
CARROLL

☆jerry
McCUE

art by

☆al
KILGORE

ABOUT COMICS | CAMARILLO, CALIFORNIA

Saints Alive!
Originally published by Abbey Books, 1953
About Comics edition published September, 2018

The characters and situations in this work are wholly fictional and imaginative; do not portray, and are not intended to portray, any actual persons or parties.

Customized editions available

Send all queries to *questions@aboutcomics.com*

SISTER
BERNADETTE

SISTER
CECILIA

MONSIGNOR
O'MALLEY

The Characters
APPEARING IN THIS BOOK

•

MOTHER
ANGELICA

The Originators

MARGARET CARROLL *and* JERRY MCCUE creators of "Convent Belles" are also the creators of the characters, gags, and situations in this book.

•

MRS. O'LEARY

The Artist

AL KILGORE

FATHER FLYNN

The Staff

ANITA MAY RYAN................*Ecclesiastical Research*
GIAN FILIPPO CIARA-MELLE....*Technical Advisor*
OSCAR HALSTED..................................*Compilation*
HUGH MONTGOMERY.............................*Production*
ISABELLA HANLEY......................................*Publicity*

TRUANT OFFICER
CLANCY

ROCCO AND RILEY

BROTHER
AMBROSE

HOBSON

OFFICER
MULLIGAN

O'FLAHERTY

3

To
Alfie, Johnny and Kew

° "I HEAR YOUR UNCLE BIM IS SUFFERING FROM
GAS TROUBLE!!"
° "YEAH, HE LIT HIS PIPE IN THE GARAGE!"

"NOW WHAT??"

- "SPACE RIDER XB 1-6-2 REPORTING"
- "WELL, RIDE BACK TO EARTH FAST, IT'S 9-0-5 A.M."

∘ "THEY'RE SO IDENTICAL, HOW CAN YOU TELL THEM APART?"
∘ "SIMPLE, ONE IS LEFT HANDED THE OTHER RIGHT, WHEN IN DOUBT I JUST THROW A PIECE OF CHALK!"

° "NOW THINK ··· IF YOU HAD 12 APPLES AND YOU
  TOOK AWAY 9, WHAT WOULD YOU HAVE LEFT?"
° "JUST ENOUGH FOR 3 LITTLE STRUDELS!"

"LA SOCIÉTÉ EST BASÉE SUR UN ÉCHANGE DE SERVICES"

°"MA, WAS ANYBODY FROM SCHOOL HERE
LOOKIN' FER ME?"
°"NO – BUT THERE WAS FOR JOHN RILEY, SR!"

"MA, DO YOU MIND IF I BRING HOME SOME
OF MY SCHOOL MATES TO PLAY WITH ME?"
"NOT AT ALL, — WHO ARE THEY?"
"NANCY O'ROURKE!"

"ISN'T YER SCHOOL THAT-A-WAY, GENTLEMEN?"
"YER RIGHT, MR. MULLIGAN, WE HAD SOMETHING ELSE ON OUR MINDS!!"

"GEORGE WASHINGTON CARVER FOUND MANY INDUSTRIAL USES FOR OUR AMERICAN PEANUT— FER INSTANCE — PEANUT BRITTLE, PEANUT CRUNCH, CHOCOLATE COATED PEANUTS, PEANUT BUTTER BARS AND SALTED PEANUTS!"

"DON'T LET THAT COLLAR FOOL YOU — HE
CAN SURE USE HIS DUKES!!"

• " . . . AND WHERE DOES OUR BEST SALMON COME FROM?"
• "THE A & P !!"

° "MY UNCLE BIM GOT A PRETTY LIVELY JOB,
   AT LAST!"
°° "YEAH, DOIN' WHAT?"
° "CLEANIN' EELS AT THE FISH MARKET!!"

"CAN YOU UNDERSTAND WHAT LITTLE BROTHER IS SAYING, JUNIOR?"

"YEAH, HE SEZ, 'WHY DO YA WASTE YOUR HARD-EARNED DOUGH ON SUCH LOUSY STUFF AS SPINACH?'"

"DON'T THEM WHITE AND BLACK KEYS REMIND
YOU OF A LOT OF TEETH WITH CAVITIES IN
THEM, PERFESSER?"

"I'VE BROUGHT THE FIFE AND DRUM CORPS
HOME TO REHEARSE, MA — BUT YOU AND
POP DON'T HAVE TO LISTEN!"

"MAYBE WE COULD USE HIM TO MAKE THE
OPPOSIN' PITCHER SICK!"

"SLIDE, MONSIGNOR, SLIDE!!"

"HERE, HERE, WHAT'S ALL THIS MESS FOR?"
"WE'RE HAVIN' A PET SHOW AT SCHOOL AND WE
DON'T WANT KATHY KELLY'S FANCY POODLE
TO THINK BOZO'S GOT FLEAS!"

"TONY SENT ME!"

•• "HE'S NOT MUCH TO LOOK AT, BUT THEY STAY
    CLEAR OF HIM IN ACTION!"
 • "WHY?"
•• "THEY'RE SCARED OF HIS BITE!!"

"DON'T MIND ME, MONSIGNOR, TODAY'S FRIDAY!"

"NAW YA DON'T, FATHER FLYNN, NO SNITCHIN'
COOKIES FROM THE PANTRY!"

° "GLAD TO HAVE YOU JOIN US, BROTHER AMBROSE
NOW WHAT IS IT YOU PARTICULARLY EXCELL IN?"
° "WELL, I SHOOT IN THE LOW EIGHTIES AND THAT'S
CONSIDERED PRETTY GOOD GOLF FOR AN AMATEUR!"

o "WHY ARE THE LIMA BEANS SO CLOSE TO THE CORN?"
o "THAT'S THE WAY SUCCOTASH IS GROWN, MOTHER!"

"MOTHER SUPERIOR WAS WONDERING WHY YOU STOPPED RINGING!"

"LIVER-R-R-R-R"

"MATCH THIS"

"BUT, IT'S YOUR HUSBAND, MRS. CLANCY, AND HE'S BROUGHT YOU FLOWERS!"

"I'M AMAZED, HE MUST HAVE BEEN TO A WAKE LAST NIGHT!"

"NOTHING SERIOUS FATHER — THE CEILING CAME DOWN ON THE GILHOOLEYS, UPSTAIRS, AND THEY'RE WAITIN' FER TH' INSURANCE ADJUSTER!"

"NO THANKS, EVERYBODY'S GOT ONE, EXCEPT MONSIGNOR—AND HE CAN'T USE ONE !!"

○ "WE'RE THE COMMITTEE TO SEE MONSIGNOR ABOUT THE PICNIC"
○ "THIS IS NO TIME FOR A PICNIC—FIRST, MONSIGNOR IS WORKING ON THE SCHOOL BUDGET AND SECOND, HIS ULCERS ARE WORKING ON HIM !!"

41

"I WAS RIGHT HERE WAITIN' FOR MY MASTER, BUT WHERE WERE YOU LAST SUNDAY, SINNER ??"

° "JUST THE GUY I WANTED TO SEE! THE CELLAR
  NEEDS CLEANIN', THE LAWN NEEDS MOWIN', THERE'S
  PLENTY TO DO... THEN I'LL FEED YOU!"

° "SO, WHOSE HUNGRY?"

"WHY DON'TCHA STOP COMIN' AROUND — YOU KNOW YOU CHURCH MICE AIN'T GOT NOTHIN'"

° "WHAT'S THE SCORE, MISTER?"
° "FER YOU AND ME LADS — IT'S THREE STRIKES!"

"LOOK, OFFICER – LET'S NOT STAND HERE AND ARGUE – THERE'S FLOWER POTS UP THERE AND I DON'T TRUST THIS CARTOONIST!!"

o "YES, OF COURSE, THE BED AND MEALS ARE
   FREE – ALL WE ASK IS A LITTLE WORK IN RETURN"
o "SOMEBODY GIVE ME A BUM STEER!"

"HAVE YOU FORGOTTEN DR. MULLARKY'S WORDS
ABOUT FRUSTRATING A CHILD? — BESIDES YOU
CAN ALWAYS BUY NEW PIPES!!"

"PASS IT UP MONSIGNOR, HE PLAYED FIRST BASE AT COLLEGE!!"

"MILD, WITH NO UNPLEASANT AFTERTASTE—**BALONEY!**"

o "CAN YOU NAME TWO VERY COMMON FARM ANI-
MALS AND SOME END PRODUCTS DERIVED FROM
THEM ?"

o "PIGS N' CHICKENS – END PRODUCTS – HAM N' EGGS"

"THIS IS THE TIME CLANCY GOES BY— LET'S HIDE
IN THE TREE"

° "CAN I TRY MY LUCK, MA'AM"
° "THAT WAY TO THE RING TOSS GAME, ME LAD!"

"CLANCY SURE LOVES THAT TREE!"

"NOW DO YA SEE WHY I OILED THE SPRINGBOARD?"

"–AND THAT MULLIGAN, ME FRIEND, IS **YOUR** TICKET TO PERDITION– IT HAPPENS TO BE THE BISHOP'S CAR!"

"BE YE NOT ALARMED, MY BRETHREN,'TIS BUT
MRS. O'LEARY'S BISCUITS TAKING
ETHEREAL FORM"

° "LET'S TAKE A ROW, HUH?"
° "WHAT- WITHOUT LIFE PRESERVERS?"

"PSYCHOLOGICALLY SPEAKIN', BROTHER AMBROSE,
WHICH SIGN CARRIES THE MOST SIGNIFICANCE?"

"IF I ONLY HAD THE TIME!!"

°"MONSIGNOR, I HAVE A DRASTIC CONFESSION
   TO MAKE, AND I HOPE YOU DON'T MIND!"
°°"GO RIGHT AHEAD, DOCTOR"
  °"I THINK I PULLED THE WRONG TOOTH (GULP!)!"

"HOW DOES THE COLOR STRIKE YOU, MONSIGNOR?"

o "I'M GOING TO THAT MISSION IN THE HIGH ALPS!!"
o "FROM WHAT I'VE HEARD OF YOUR SINGING —
   YODELING FOR YOU IS A NATURAL!!!"

"OF COURSE, I REMEMBERED THE BISHOP WAS COMIN', BUT WITH PRICES SO HIGH — IT HAD TO BE HASH!!"

◦ "YOU'RE LATE, FATHER FLYNN, YOU MUST'VE
HAD A BIG DAY!!"
◦ "SURE DID, THEY TIED THE SCORE IN THE 9TH
AND THE GAME WENT 12 INNINGS!!!"

"IN REPLY TO MANY INQUIRIES, THE STRANGE SOUNDS EMANATING FROM OUR CHURCH, TUESDAY NIGHTS, ARE FROM OUR CHOIR— IN REHEARSAL!"

"THERE IS NOTHING SO INVIGORATING AS THE SMELL OF BURNING AUTUMN LEAVES!"

"WADDA YA MEAN, GO BACK FOR HOT TEA?
THIS HAS BEEN STANDARD EQUIPMENT
UP HERE FOR YEARS!!"

"WELL, I SEE YOU HAD GOOD LUCK, MY BOY.
WHERE DID YOU CATCH THAT EXCELLANT FISH?"
"OVER AT GILHOOLEY'S FISH MARKET!"

○ "ANOTHER "A" TEST ??!! "
○ "NO, PADRE — SMOKE SIGNAL — SQUAW HEAD
MAD — SHE SAY, 'COME HOME AT ONCE' "

" YA CAN'T BE TOO SURE !! "

"TRY A SAMBA – AND LET'S SEE WHAT HAPPENS!!"

"CERTAINLY NOT WHILE THEY'RE WORKING
LIKE TWO LITTLE BEAVERS, MR. CLANCY!!"

"AW NO ⋯⋯ IT COULDN'T BE !"

"IT SAYS HERE — 'LOCK ALL WINDOWS AND DOORS
SECURELY, LIGHT SULPHUR CANDLE, PLACE IN
CENTER OF FLOOR AND LEAVE THE HOUSE—
GUARANTEED ALL PESTS WILL BE EXTERMINATED'
WELL, ALL WE GOTTA DO NOW IS LIGHT IT AND GO!"

"*Psst!* Have you seen today's *Daily Nun*??"

Classic Catholic
Cartoon Collections
FROM ABOUT COMICS

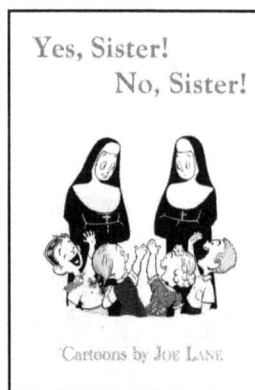

Look for them
where you got this book,
or visit www.AboutComics.com

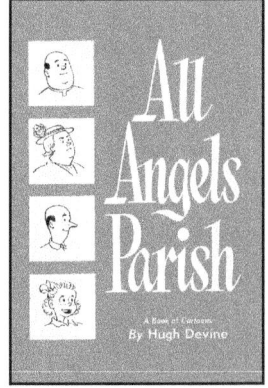

Five books worth of nun cartoons in one bargain volume!

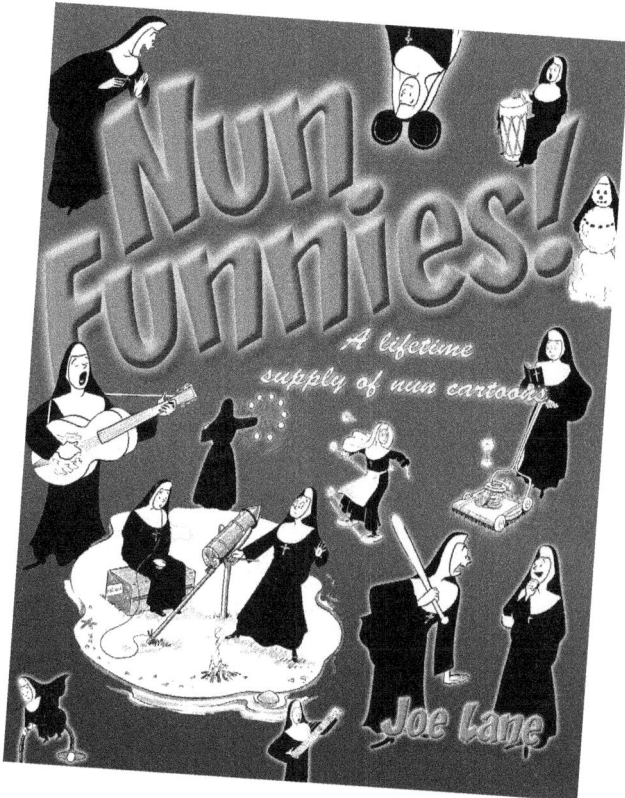

www.ingramcontent.com/pod-product-compliance
Lightning Source LLC
Chambersburg PA
CBHW071835020426
42331CB00007B/1739